Prayer... the Key to Unlocking Blessings

12 Days of Prayer and Fasting

Mary A. Ford

Publisher. by lisabell
Radical Women
(DBA)
PO Box 782
Granbury, TX
76048
www.bylisabell.com

ISBN-10: 0-9983308-8-4
ISBN-13: 978-0-9983308-8-4

DEDICATION

This book, *Prayer: The Key to Unlocking Blessings* is dedicated to my soulmate and husband, Rev. James A. Ford for being my #1 Prayer Partner over the years of our marriage. Thank you, for being my friend, confidant and the priest of our home.

Mary A. Ford

Mary A. Ford

Table of Contents

INTRODUCTION

At the beginning of each New Year, my husband and I seek the Lord's direction concerning our lives and ministry through a dedicated time of prayer and fasting together. As we began to wind down one particular year, the Lord resonated the number twelve (12) in my spirit. As I prayed and contemplated on this number, and its significant biblical meanings, I began to reflect on various times of joy and pain in our lives over the past year. Even though some of the times were sorrowful, I could still see God's hand in every circumstance.

Although I was aware that the number 12 had significant biblical meaning, the Lord led me to research this number further. The number 12 is a combination of the number "1," which means, *"stay positive,"* and the number "2," which means, *"keep the faith"*. When combined together to form the number 12, it sends a strong message that no matter what occurs in life the coming year—stay positive, optimistic, and filled with faith! After all, it's not *what* you go through—it's *how* you go through it.

This is a significant message of courage and hope for all believers. Your positive thoughts, attitude, faith and prayers, coupled with fasting, will create positive outcomes in your life! As Christians, Jesus is our ultimate example—every day, and in every way! Jesus fasted and prayed for forty (40) days prior to launching out into His public ministry (Luke 4:2). Although Jesus' ministry was only for three and a half years, it would have a profound impact on not only the people of His day, but for innumerable others down through the decades until present day—and beyond!

So as believers, we too must follow Jesus' example as we launch out into a new year, new ministry, new territory, or a new way of life. Having a *desire* for things to change in you, through you, and around you will take more than just wishful thinking—some things will only come by way of fervent prayer and fasting (Daniel 9:3). Therefore, as you commit to fasting and praying for the next 12 days for loved ones to be delivered, strongholds to be broken, the lost to be saved, broken relationships mended, failed marriages restored, wayward children returned home and back to God, debts cancelled, finances restored, the sick healed, and so much more, look for the miraculous to happen—the saints will be edified and God will be glorified!

Yes—these positive outcomes, and many more unimaginable, will occur when believers stand on God's promises in steadfast prayer and fasting. If believers truly want to get involved in God's Kingdom building agenda, they must become concerned about the things that concern God. Praying for the unchurched and unsaved become a top priority in Kingdom building work, and *"The Great Commission"* will then become a passion instead of a possibility for the believer to seek after and fulfill.

Do you desire to see a mighty move of God in your life, the lives of others, the nation and around the world? Then for the next 12 days, commit to praying and fasting for 12-hours each day, between the hours of 7:00AM—7:00PM. An *absolute* or *complete* fast is recommended—meaning no food or liquids consumed during the 12-hour fasting period. However, for those who may have a medical condition, water is permissible and a *Daniel Fast* or *Modified Fast* under a physician's guidance is highly recommended.

This book contains twelve (12) specific scripture-based *Prayer Focuses*—one for each of the *12 Days of Prayer and Fasting*. Each prayer focus contains several *Prayer Points* to guide you through your personal prayer time and throughout the day; including dedicated pages to journal your personal prayers and capture spiritual insights for specific needs—all based on the prayer focus of the day. There are also sample prayers included for each day to encourage you along the way.

But remember…the purpose of spiritual fasting is not to lose weight, rather to *"gain"* a closer walk with God. Fasting 12-hours for 12-days is not about proving holiness, but rather a dedicated time set aside each day to humbly submit oneself in prayer to the Father—thoughts, speech, actions, attitude and will—totally surrendered to God. As you pray and fast for renewal, restoration and spiritual revival in your personal life, home, schools, churches, community, government, nation and the world—great and miraculous things will begin to happen! (Jeremiah 33:3). Most of all, you will find yourself drawing closer to God as you humbly seek His face in fervent prayer—trusting Him to do the impossible and committing every area of your life into His capable care. As you submit and surrender your will to God's will, He will hear your prayers, forgive your sin, and heal the land!

"If my people, who are called by my name, will humble themselves and pray and seek my face and turn from their wicked ways, then I will hear from heaven, and I will forgive their sin and will heal their land." (2 Chronicles 7:14)

ENJOY YOUR JOURNEY!

Mary A. Ford

COMMITMENT

I commit to praying and fasting for the next twelve (12) days, for twelve (12) hours each day, between 7:00AM and 7:00PM.

Signature	*Date*

Day 1

Prayer Focus
SALVATION OF THE LOST AND UNCHURCHED
(Pray name by name for those you know to be unsaved or unchurched)

Support Scriptures
Luke 8:5-15; Matthew 13:15; Matthew 9:37-38

Pray for...

- ✦ The hearts of the lost and unchurched to be changed; and the unsaved to come into the saving grace of Jesus Christ.
- ✦ The spiritual eyes and ears of the unsaved and unchurched to be opened to the truths of Christ and God's word regarding every area of life.
- ✦ The lost to have God's attitude toward sin and to be released to believe in faith.
- ✦ The saved to truly desire a transformed life in Christ and to go into the harvest field to share Christ, serve and disciple others.

Spiritual Insight

(Write on the lines below what God is speaking to your heart)

_____

_____

_____

_____

_____

_____

_____

_____

_____

_____

_____

_____

_____

_____

_____

_____

_____

_____

_____

_____

Journal Your Personal Prayer

In Jesus' name I pray, Amen.

Father God, I pray that all Christians will remember with humble gratitude what they have been saved from; representing our Savior well in interactions with others, and having a heart drawn to prayer for those unsaved and unchurched. Father, turn hearts back to you so that spiritual eyes and ears are opened to the truth of Christ, and hearts are surrendered to God's word regarding every area of life—sincerely having your attitude towards sin. Help those who are saved to truly desire and live a transformed life in Christ— going into the harvest field to share Christ, serve others and disciple the saved. In Jesus' saving name I pray—Amen.

Day 2

Prayer Focus
OUR NATION ~ STOP, DROP & PRAY 4-USA!
(Pray for our military, government, administrating bodies, and nation)

Support Scriptures
I Timothy 2:1-4; Zechariah 4:6; Ezra 9:6; Psalm 51:16-17

Pray for...

- Blessings upon the USA and for strength, wisdom and spiritual guidance for our president, vice president and all other governing authorities.
- The United States government, armed forces and military troops to have support strengthened as well as for retired veterans.
- Jobs, health care and housing for those in need.
- Restoration of safety, love, respect and peaceful demonstrations of differences within our communities and nation.
- The peace of Jerusalem and Israel, peace in the Middle East, and abolishment of terrorism—both foreign and domestic.
- God's people and our national leaders will not trust in military strength, financial might, human strategies or political power and influence to solve our difficulties, but return to the scriptures to guide our decision-making so that our nation may once again become "One Nation Under God."

Spiritual Insight

(Write on the lines below what God is speaking to your heart)

_____

_____

_____

_____

_____

_____

_____

_____

_____

_____

_____

_____

_____

_____

_____

_____

_____

_____

_____

_____

_____

Journal Your Personal Prayer

_____

_____

_____

_____

_____

_____

_____

_____

_____

_____

_____

_____

_____

_____

_____

_____

_____

_____

_____

_____

In Jesus' name I pray, Amen.

Father God, bless these United States of America. Endow our President, Vice President and all other governing authorities with knowledge and wisdom to make sound decisions that will impact the nation and people for the good. Father, we pray that same spirit of wisdom will guide our mayor's, governors, judges, and legal authorities. Lord, bless those in need of jobs, health care and housing. Restore the safety, love, respect and peaceful environments within our communities and nation. Protect and cover our armed forces and military troops and provide what is needed to retired veterans. Father, we also Pray for the peace of Jerusalem and Israel, peace in Middle East, and the abolishment of terrorism— both foreign and domestic. Lord, help your people and national leaders to not put their trust in military strength, financial might, human strategies or political power and influence to solve our difficulties. Rather, help those in authority to return to the scriptures to guide decision-making so that our nation may once again become "One Nation under God." In the name of Jesus I pray—Amen.

Day 3

Prayer Focus
PRAYERS FOR CHRISTIAN FAMILIES & HOMES
(Pray for every member of your family—name by name)

Support Scriptures
Galatians 6:1; 2 Chronicles 7:15; Acts1:14

Pray for...

- Every member of your home to honor God and prioritize corporate worship together.
- Family devotion and prayer time to be restored and prioritized in all Christian homes.
- Good family and friend relationships based upon godly principles.
- Humble and forgiving spirits among family members.
- Reunited families and restoration of broken relationships.
- Christian families to model Christ and be a positive influence within the community.

Spiritual Insight

(Write on the lines below what God is speaking to your heart)

Journal Your Personal Prayer

_____

_____

_____

_____

_____

_____

_____

_____

_____

_____

_____

_____

_____

_____

_____

_____

_____

_____

_____

_____

In Jesus' name I pray, Amen.

Father God, I pray for members of Christian families to honor God and prioritize the study of God's word, prayer and worship together. I pray that family devotion and prayer time be restored and prioritized in all Christian homes. Father, I pray for broken relationships to be mended and new God-centered relationships formed. I pray good family and friend relationships based upon godly principles are developed; and give us humble and forgiving spirits towards one another that will reunite families and restore broken relationships. Father, help Christian families model Christ and be a positive influence within the community. In Jesus' name I pray, Amen.

Day 4

Prayer Focus
CHILDREN, YOUTH, YOUNG ADULTS, SCHOOLS AND ADMINISTRATORS
(Pray for the children, youth and young adults you know name by name)

Support Scriptures
1 Peter 5:5-10; 1 Corinthians 6:18; Proverbs 22:6; Acts 17:27-28

Pray for...

+ Children, youth and young adults to be clothed in humility, respectful to elders and one another, and exhibit proper behavior at all times—always lifting their concerns up to God in prayer and trusting Him to exalt them in due season.
+ Children, youth and young adults to remain sexually pure and for their salvation at an early age.
+ God to raise up godly leaders in our children, youth and young adults so they will obey God and represent Him well in all arenas of life.
+ Godly parents who will train up their children in the Word— dedicating them to the Lord at an early age and setting a pattern of seeking the Lord in all things so that the younger generations may find strength and hope in the Lord.
+ Godly school administrators, principals, teachers and support staff.
+ God to be brought back into our schools, colleges, and universities around the county and world.

Spiritual Insight

(Write on the lines below what God is speaking to your heart)

_____

_____

_____

_____

_____

_____

_____

_____

_____

_____

_____

_____

_____

_____

_____

_____

_____

_____

_____

_____

Journal Your Personal Prayer

_____

_____

_____

_____

_____

_____

_____

_____

_____

_____

_____

_____

_____

_____

_____

_____

_____

_____

_____

_____

In Jesus' name I pray, Amen.

Father God, I come praying for the children, youth and young adults—that they will be clothed in humility, respectful to elders and one another, exhibit proper behavior at all times, and always lift their concerns up to you in prayer. I pray that they trust you to exalt them in due season, that they remain sexually pure, and that they come to know you through salvation at an early age. Father, raise up godly leaders in our children that will obey your word and represent you well in all arenas of life. I Pray for godly school administrators, principals, teachers and support staff, and that God be brought back into our schools, colleges, and universities. Father, I Pray for godly parents who will train up their children in the Word—dedicating them to the Lord, and setting a pattern of seeking the Lord in all things so that the younger generations may find strength and hope in the name of Jesus! Hear our prayer for our children on this day, Oh Lord! It's in the righteous name of Jesus I humbly pray—Amen.

Day 5

Prayer Focus
RESTORATION OF CHRISTIAN MARRIAGES
(Pray for your marriage and all other married couples you know name by name)

Support Scriptures
Ephesians 5:22-33; 1 Peter 3: 1-2, 7; Hebrews 13:4; 1 Peter 3:7-12

Pray for...

+ God to raise up and restore Christian marriages—with husbands and wives willing to do it God's way and not their own; resulting in a decline in the divorce rate.
+ Husbands to love the Lord with their whole hearts and love their wives like Christ loves the church.
+ Husbands to be the providers, heads of households, divine leaders, and loving and affectionate priests of their own homes.
+ Wives to support, encourage, respect and submit to their own husbands as unto the Lord; and trust the God in their husbands to lead as Christ would lead.
+ Husbands and wives to commit to praying together and consistently studying God's word together in order to cultivate an atmosphere of love, respect and peace in their home.
+ Oneness, unity, commitment, unconditional love and the sanctity of the bedroom in marriages.
+ Selflessness and forgiveness within marriages, and that husbands and wives will be humble in spirit so that their prayers may be heard.

Spiritual Insight

(Write on the lines below what God is speaking to your heart)

_____

_____

_____

_____

_____

_____

_____

_____

_____

_____

_____

_____

_____

_____

_____

_____

_____

_____

_____

_____

Journal Your Personal Prayer

_____

_____

_____

_____

_____

_____

_____

_____

_____

_____

_____

_____

_____

_____

_____

_____

_____

_____

_____

_____

In Jesus' name I pray, Amen.

Father God, raise up Christian marriages and decrease divorce rates in homes around the world. Bless husbands and wives with forgiving hearts and a desire to do it "God's way" and not their own. Help husbands to love the Lord with their whole hearts and love their wives like Christ loves the church. Bless and enable husbands to be the providers, heads of households, divine leaders, and loving and affectionate priests of their own homes. Father, I Pray that wives will support, encourage, respect and submit to their own husbands as unto the Lord with joy; and trust the God in their husbands to lead as Christ would lead. Lord, Help husbands and wives to commit to praying together and to consistently study God's word together in order to cultivate an atmosphere of love, respect and peace in their home. Allow oneness, unity, commitment, and unconditional love to rule and reign over and within the bedroom of Christian marriages. Most of all, let selflessness and forgiveness be abundant and allow husbands and wives to show humility of spirit in all they do so that their prayers may not be hindered. It's in the name of Jesus I humbly pray—Amen.

Day 6

Prayer Focus
MENTAL AND SPIRITUAL DELIVERANCE & BREAKING OF STRONGHOLDS

(Pray for those you know who are under satanic attack or need deliverance— name by name)

Support Scriptures
2 Corinthians 10:3-5; Ephesians 5:1-7; Jude 1:7; 1 Timothy 4:1-2

Pray for...

+ Deliverance from satanic attacks—emotional, mental and spiritual warfare and breaking of specific strongholds.
+ Deliverance from demonic possession, suppression and oppression.
+ Deliverance from various chemical addictions, perverse behaviors and sin nature.
+ Deliverance from stress, anxiety, depression and other mental disorders.
+ Deliverance from foul language, sexual sins, pornography, and gay and lesbian behaviors.

Spiritual Insight

(Write on the lines below what God is speaking to your heart)

_____

_____

_____

_____

_____

_____

_____

_____

_____

_____

_____

_____

_____

_____

_____

_____

_____

_____

_____

_____

_____

_____

Journal Your Personal Prayer

_____

_____

_____

_____

_____

_____

_____

_____

_____

_____

_____

_____

_____

_____

_____

_____

_____

_____

_____

In Jesus' name I pray, Amen.

Father God, I come praying for those under satanic attack— emotional, mental and spiritual warfare. I pray for the breaking of strongholds that bind so many of your people. Free those under demonic possession, suppression and oppression; and those needing deliverance from various addictions and sinful habits. Father, I lift up to you those needing deliverance from stress, anxiety and depression, including deliverance from foul language and sexual sins such as pornography, and gay and lesbian behaviors. I plead the blood of Jesus over every condition, situation and person needing a spiritual breakthrough...In Jesus' Name, Amen!

Day 7

Prayer Focus
PHYSICAL HEALTH AND HEALING
(Pray for those who are sick, diseased or need physical or psychological healing)

Support Scriptures
James 5:13-16; Luke 4:18

Pray for...

+ Physical, emotional, and mental health and wellness of those in need.
+ Those sick at home, in hospitals, rehabilitation facilities and nursing homes—healing, recovery, comfort and restoration.
+ Healing of specific sickness and diseases—cancer, diabetes, HIV/AIDS, hypertension, heart, kidney, etc.
+ Healing of addictive behaviors—smoking, alcohol, drugs, obesity, anorexia, etc.

Spiritual Insight

(Write on the lines below what God is speaking to your heart)

_____

_____

_____

_____

_____

_____

_____

_____

_____

_____

_____

_____

_____

_____

_____

_____

_____

_____

_____

_____

_____

_____

Journal Your Personal Prayer

_____

_____

_____

_____

_____

_____

_____

_____

_____

_____

_____

_____

_____

_____

_____

_____

_____

_____

_____

_____

In Jesus' name I pray, Amen.

Father God, I come praying for the physical, emotional, and mental health and wellness of those in need. Touch those sick at home, in hospitals and in other long-term care facilities with your healing power. Allow them to feel your love and give them peace of mind and comfort in knowing you are working on their behalf. Release your healing power, allowing complete recovery and restoration within and throughout their bodies, according to your will. I pray and plead the blood of Jesus over those suffering and in need of healing from specific sickness and diseases—cancer, lupus, heart conditions, diabetes, HIV/AIDS, blood pressure issues, digestive disorders, kidney and other major organ malfunctions. Father, I also pray for the healing of perverseness and addictive behaviors—smoking, alcohol, drugs, obesity, anorexia, pornography, and others that plague, deteriorate and destroy these physical temples and prohibits a closer walk with you! Hear our cry, Oh Lord, and heal your people...in the name of Jesus! Amen

Prayer Focus
STEWARDSHIP AND FINANCIAL RELEASE
(Pray for your personal financial stewardship and for others who are in need)

Support Scriptures
Haggai 2:8; Matthew 25:14-30; Malachi 3:8; Deut 12:6; Romans 14:12; Galatians 2:7; Proverbs 13:11; Matthew 22:17-21; 1 Tim 6:10

Pray for...

+ Willingness to trust God completely with personal finances and possessions over which you have been given stewardship.
+ Faithfulness in giving tithes and offerings; and in giving of first fruits to the Lord.
+ Willingness and obedience to be a good steward of the gifts and talents God has given you; and to use those gifts and talents for the edification of the saints, evangelism of sinners and building up of the Kingdom for Christ.
+ Honorable business ethics, godly partnerships, and investments and money management practices that will glorify God.
+ Believers to be released from financial bondage and become wise stewards of all financial blessings so that they might "be a blessing" to others in need.

Spiritual Insight

(Write on the lines below what God is speaking to your heart)

_____

_____

_____

_____

_____

_____

_____

_____

_____

_____

_____

_____

_____

_____

_____

_____

_____

_____

_____

_____

_____

_____

_____

_____

_____

_____

Journal Your Personal Prayer

_____

_____

_____

_____

_____

_____

_____

_____

_____

_____

_____

_____

_____

_____

_____

_____

_____

_____

_____

In Jesus' name I pray, Amen.

Father God, help your children to trust you completely with their finances and possessions—realizing you have given them stewardship over these things. Help them to be faithful in giving tithes and offerings—giving of first fruits to the Lord with joy! Give your children the desire to honor you in all business dealings, partnerships, investments, and other financial matters; and help them to also be good stewards of their God-given gifts and talents—using them for the edification of the saints, evangelism of sinners and building up of the Kingdom for Christ. I pray that all believers will be released from financial bondage and become wise stewards of all financial blessings in order that they might be a blessing to others in need. In Jesus' name I pray and give you praise—Amen.

Day 9

Prayer Focus
PASTORS AND CHURCHES

(Pray for your pastor and first family. Pray for all pastors and churches globally)

Support Scriptures
Ephesians 4:11-13; Isaiah 56:1-7; Jeremiah 23:1-4; Luke 18:1;
Philippians 4:6-7; Matthew 21:13

Pray for...

+ Christian's being persecuted around the world, and that their right to openly exercise Christianity without fear of retaliation be upheld.
+ All pastors to boldly stand and preach the uncompromised gospel and saving grace of Jesus Christ.
+ Direction, protection, guidance and encouragement of your pastor and for all pastors truly exhibiting and supporting Kingdom agendas.
+ Church leadership, staff, ministry members and volunteers to serve as unto the Lord and seek His guidance in every area of service and ministry.
+ Churches around the world to be revived and spiritually on fire for the Lord—truly demonstrating the unconditional Agape love of Christ.
+ God's wisdom to rest upon pastors as they call their congregations into intercession and lead them to an understanding of the times.
+ A spirit of prayer to spread like wildfire across homes, churches and the land until every church becomes a "House of Prayer," saturated with seasons and extended times of turning to the Lord.

(Write on the lines below what God is speaking to your heart)

Journal Your Personal Prayer

_____

_____

_____

_____

_____

_____

_____

_____

_____

_____

_____

_____

_____

_____

_____

_____

_____

_____

_____

_____

In Jesus' name I pray, Amen.

Father God, I come lifting up Christians all around the world...praying against persecution and the ability to openly exercise Christian beliefs without fear of retaliation. I pray that all pastors will boldly stand and preach the un-compromised gospel and share the truth of Christ's saving grace. I pray for direction, protection, guidance and encouragement of all pastors—give angels charge over those who are truly exhibiting and supporting Kingdom agendas. Father, help church leadership, staff, ministry leaders/members, and volunteers to serve "as unto the Lord" and seek your guidance in every area of work, service and ministry. Father, give pastors wisdom as they call their congregations to intercession and lead them to an understanding of the times. I pray for a "spirit of prayer" to spread like wildfire across our homes, churches and land until every church truly becomes a "House of Prayer", saturated with seasons and extended times of turning to the Lord. I pray for true REVIVAL to take place in all churches around the world—setting congregations on spiritual fire for the Lord—truly demonstrating the unconditional love of Christ as they serve and worship God in spirit and truth! These things I ask in the mighty and matchless name of Jesus the Christ— Amen.

Day 10

Prayer Focus
INCARCERATED AND PRESERVATION OF LIFE
(Pray for those incarcerated and for the preservation of life and justice for all)

Support Scriptures
Ezra 7:26; Deuteronomy 28:41; Acts 5:18-20; Psalm 127:3; Deuteronomy 5:17; Galatians 3:28

Pray for...

+ Our sons and daughters to uphold the laws of God and man, and not fall prey into the prison systems of this land.
+ Rehabilitation of our criminal system and that true justice for all is restored.
+ Protection, daily guidance and spiritual and physical deliverance of those you know to be incarcerated in local jails, and state and federal prisons.
+ Unborn lives to be saved from destruction and that those desiring children will have fertile wombs, or be willing to adopt.
+ Gang-related violence and shootings to cease.
+ Senseless shootings of people of color and the slaying of police to cease.
+ People to no longer be judged by the color of their skin, but by the content of their character.

40

Spiritual Insight

(Write on the lines below what God is speaking to your heart)

_____

_____

_____

_____

_____

_____

_____

_____

_____

_____

_____

_____

_____

_____

_____

_____

_____

_____

_____

_____

_____

Journal Your Personal Prayer

_____

_____

_____

_____

_____

_____

_____

_____

_____

_____

_____

_____

_____

_____

_____

_____

_____

_____

_____

_____

_____

In Jesus' name I pray, Amen.

Father God, I come praying that our sons and daughters will uphold the laws of the land and God, and not fall prey into the prison systems. I pray for the rehabilitation of our criminal system and that true justice for all be restored. I pray that unborn lives will be saved from destruction and those desiring children will have fertile wombs or be led to adopt. Father, I pray that gang-related shootings will cease and that the senseless shootings of people of color and the slaying of police will cease. I pray that people will no longer be judged by the color of their skin, but the content of their character. I pray these things in the precious name of Jesus—Amen

Day 11

Prayer Focus
PERSONAL AND CHURCH-WIDE SPIRITUAL GROWTH & MATURITY

(Pray for personal and church-wide spiritual growth & maturity. Name areas of growth needed)

Support Scriptures
2 Corinthians 7:9-10; Deuteronomy 6:5; John 13:34; Isaiah 26:9; Nehemiah 9:2-3; James 5:16

Pray for...

+ No longer desire milk, but the sincere meat of God's word to guide you through life.
+ Grieve over your own personal sins—then confess and repent without delay.
+ Know God better through his word and prayer—hungering and thirsting after God and His righteousness over the world.
+ Desire and commit to dedicated time spent with God in prayer and the study and application of His word.
+ Be spiritually accountable and for the Holy Spirt to fall fresh upon you, your family and the church at large.
+ Effectively serve in the church body—using your spiritual gifts and talents for mission, ministry and witness.
+ Have spirit-lead and anointed pastors, worship leaders, musicians, choirs, praise teams, staff, ministry leaders and volunteers.

Spiritual Insight

(Write on the lines below what God is speaking to your heart)

_____

_____

_____

_____

_____

_____

_____

_____

_____

_____

_____

_____

_____

_____

_____

_____

_____

_____

_____

_____

_____

Journal Your Personal Prayer

_____

_____

_____

_____

_____

_____

_____

_____

_____

_____

_____

_____

_____

_____

_____

_____

_____

_____

_____

_____

_____

In Jesus' name I pray, Amen.

Father God, I Pray that believers will seek after personal spiritual growth and maturity—no longer desiring milk, but the meat of God's word to guide their life. Help us to grieve over our own personal sins, then confess and repent. Father, help your children to know you better through your word and prayer—hungering and thirsting after your righteousness. Help us to commit to dedicating more time spent in prayer and study of your word—applying what we learn to our daily life. Lord, allow spiritual accountability and freshness to fall upon your children and the church at large. Give us the desire to effectively serve in the church body—using our spiritual gifts and talents for mission, ministry and witnessing. Father, I pray that you will raise up spirit-lead and anointed pastors, worship leaders, musicians, choirs, praise teams, church staff, ministry leaders and volunteers. Lord, REVIVE your people again! It's in the matchless name of Jesus I pray. Amen.

Day 12

Prayer Focus
HEALING OF OUR LAND! (2 CHRONICLES 7:14)
(Pray for God to hear the cry of the humble and heal our land!)

Support Scriptures
Micah 6:8; Proverbs 18:12; Matt. 6:33; Phil. 2:14-16; 4:6-7; Mark 10:27; Isaiah 59:1; Psalms 145:18; 1 John 1:9; Jeremiah 3:22; Hosea 6:1; Joel 2:25

Pray for...

+ Believers to walk in a spirit of humility; recognizing that pride leads to destruction and humility precedes honor.
+ ALL Christians to seek God first in prayer at the beginning of each day before getting involved in work or other activates.
+ Urgency and fervency to characterize the prayers of all Christians and that our first response to life situations and circumstances will be to pray—not panic!
+ Believers to seek God's face humbly and have increased faith in God's ability to intervene supernaturally in any situation—accomplishing the impossible!
+ Christians everywhere to understand the dire importance and their personal responsibility to live holy and blameless before a lost and watching world.
+ God to raise up an army of Prayer Warriors who are willing to persevere in prayer and wage war on their knees!

Praise God...

- His hand is not too short to save, His ear is not too heavy to hear our one accord prayers, and for His promise to hear and draw near to all who call upon Him in truth!
- His promise is true—to extend mercy, forgive our sin and cleanse those who confess and forsake their sins!
- He is faithful to keep His promise to heal those who have fallen away, bind up the wounds of the torn and bruised, and restore the years that the locust has eaten!

Spiritual Insight

(Write on the lines below what God is speaking to your heart)

_____

_____

_____

_____

_____

_____

_____

_____

_____

_____

_____

_____

_____

_____

_____

_____

_____

_____

_____

_____

_____

_____

Journal Your Personal Prayer

_____

_____

_____

_____

_____

_____

_____

_____

_____

_____

_____

_____

_____

_____

_____

_____

_____

_____

_____

In Jesus' name I pray, Amen.

Father God, how excellent is your name in all the earth! Please hear the humble cry of your children! Help those who believe in you to walk in a spirit of humility; recognizing that pride leads to destruction and humility precedes honor. I pray that all Christians will seek you first in prayer at the beginning of each day before getting involved in work or other activates—allowing urgency and fervency to characterize their prayers so that it will be their first response to life situations and circumstances—pray, not panic! I pray that as believers humbly seek your face, their faith will increase in your ability to intervene supernaturally in any situation and do the impossible! Father, I pray that Christians everywhere will understand the dire importance and take personal responsibility to live holy and blameless before a lost and watching world. I pray that God will raise up an army of Prayer Warriors and Prayer Intercessors who are willing to persevere in prayer and wage war on their knees! Father, I praise you because your hand is not too short to save, and your ear is not too heavy to hear our one accord prayers! I praise you for your promise to hear and draw near to all who call upon you in truth. I praise you for your promise to extend mercy, forgive our sin and cleanse those who confess and forsake their sins. And, I praise you, Oh Lord, for your promise to heal those who have fallen away, to bind up the wounds of the torn and bruised, and to restore the years that the locust has eaten! Thank You Lord, for hearing our prayers, forgiving our sin and healing our land! It's in the mighty, matchless name of Jesus I pray and praise you—Hallelujah and Amen!

ABOUT THE AUTHOR
Mary A. Ford

Author * Speaker * Teacher * Prayer Leader
For Booking Information Visit Mary's website:
www.duty2delightministries.com

Mary is a native Texan and resident of Arlington, Texas. Mary is married to Reverend James A. Ford, Jr. and they both serve in ministry together at the Koinonia Christian Church of Arlington, Texas, where she serves as the Prayer Ministry Director.

Mary is a PRAYER WARRIOR, PRAYER LEADER and a TEACHER of God's WORD, having taught various classes and workshops on scripture based prayer for over 20 years. Mary has served as presenter, session speaker and prayer leader for various marriage conferences, women's conferences, prayer breakfasts and prayer revivals. Together with her husband, Mary has conducted workshops on "Intimacy and Oneness" and "Praying Together to Stay Together" as a husband-wife team.

Whether FACILITATING a workshop, TEACHING a class, SPEAKING at a conference or conducting THE PRAYER FUELING STATION, Mary expels such fervor, passion, enthusiasm, and conviction while moving audiences to embrace change through being hearers and doers. She captivates her audience while moving them to bring about positive, life-altering results in their lives.

Mary's workshops, sessions and classes on prayer have been described as INTERACTIVE, ENGAGING, MOTIVATIONAL, ENCOURAGING, and LIFE CHANGING. Participants leave equipped and encouraged to truly seek a more intimate relationship with God through prayer—thus moving their prayer life "From Duty to Delight!"

OTHER BOOKS BY MARY A. FORD

⚜ *"From Duty to Delight: Are You Enjoying Jesus Yet?"*
This is a 52 week scripture-based encouragement devotional divinely designed to inspire spiritual growth, uplift your spirit, strengthen your resolve, and encourage a transformed walk with Christ!

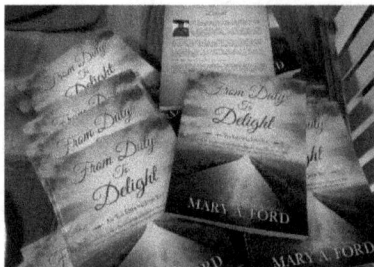

⚜ *"Hour of Power: Moving Your Prayer Life to the Next Level"*
This scripture-based study guide on prayer will encourage Christians to cultivate a more powerful, purposeful and effective prayer life through spending dedicated, consistent, intimate time with the lover of their souls—*and truly enjoy it!*

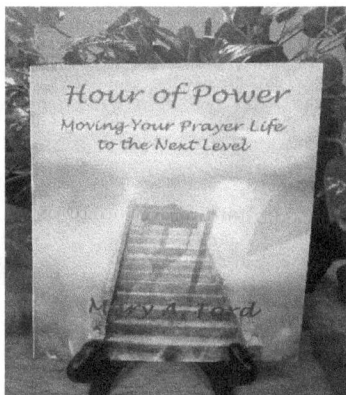

www.ingramcontent.com/pod-product-compliance
Lightning Source LLC
Chambersburg PA
CBHW071735020426
42331CB00008B/2036